JOHN LESLEY
CONTINENTS OF THE WORLD
Europe
AF583438
REDBACK publishing

Europe

Wildlife Wonders p.24

Special Places in Europe p.26

Redback Publishing
Suite 6, 13a Narabang Way,
Belrose NSW 2085
Australia

www.redbackpublishing.com
orders@redbackpublishing.com

ISBN 978-1-761400-98-8

Author: John Lesley
Editor: Caroline Thomas
Designer: Redback Publishing

Original illustrations © Redback Publishing 2025

Originated by Redback Publishing

Acknowledgements
Abbreviations: l—left, r—right, b—bottom, t—top, c—centre, m—middle

We would like to thank the following for permission to reproduce photographs (images © Shutterstock unless otherwise stated): p3br, p21b Vatican City, Italy, p7br Doggerland map, Francis Lima, CC BY-SA 4.0 (https://creativecommons.org/licenses/by-sa/4.0), via Wikimedia Commons, p9bl Istanbul, Turkey, 4.murat, p9br London, UK, David Steele, p16t Nato, Brussels, Belgium, Alexandros Michailidis, p16b European Union, Brussels, Belgium, Alexandros Michailidis, p17tr Nato flag, sashk0, p19b Eyjafjallajokull, Iceland, Johann Helgason, p20br Dubrovnik, Croatia, Solarisys, p22bl restaurant, Dubrovnik, Croatia, paul prescott, p26bl, p32br Stonehenge, UK, Drone Explorer

A catalogue record for this book is available from the National Library of Australia

Contents

Europe's Economy p.22

The People of Europe p.20

Earth's 7 Continents

Or are there 5?

Some people group Europe and Asia into one continent called Eurasia, and they combine North and South America into the Americas. According to this method of counting, there are five continents instead of seven.

What is a continent?

A continent is a very large landmass that is separated from others on Earth. Some are separated by oceans, but others have land borders with each other.

Origin of Europe

How did the continents form?

The rocky surface of our planet is constantly moving in a process called plate tectonics. As massive blocks of rock separate, they move across the surface of Earth, forming the continents we know today.

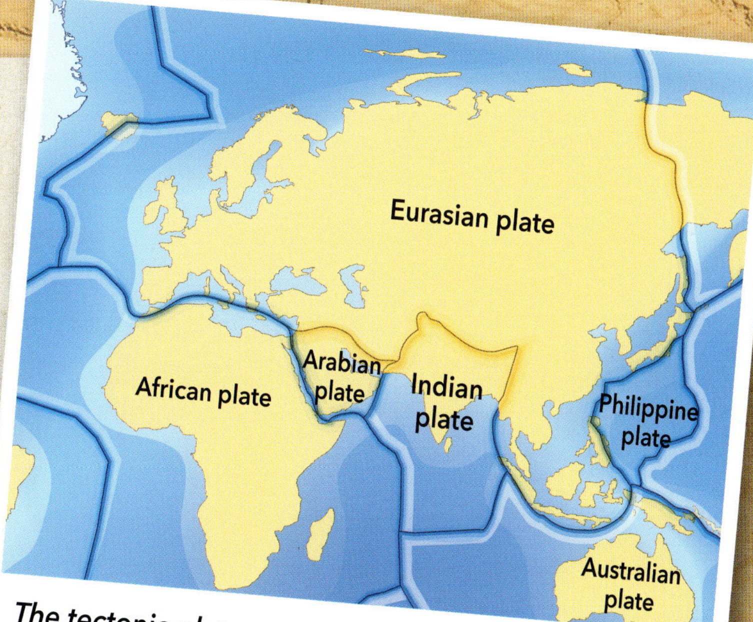

The tectonic plate on which Europe sits is still moving, but at the very slow rate of a few centimetres each year.

A Continent is Born

The continents were not always in the same location as they are now. Millions of years ago, they were parts of other huge masses of land, one of which was Laurasia, which eventually became Europe and Asia.

When Laurasia split apart, the movement resulted in the birth of the new continents of North America, Europe and parts of Asia.

Europe's Continental Shelves

The continental shelves around Europe are very large. They were probably inhabited by early groups of humans until the end of the Ice Age gradually flooded the area.

Where a continent meets the ocean, the land at the edge often continues under the water as a continental shelf. This shelf may stop abruptly at a point where the underwater rocks drop down to a deep ocean abyss.

During the last Ice Age, which ended about 10,000 years ago, some of these continental shelves were dry land, making the continents much bigger than they are today.

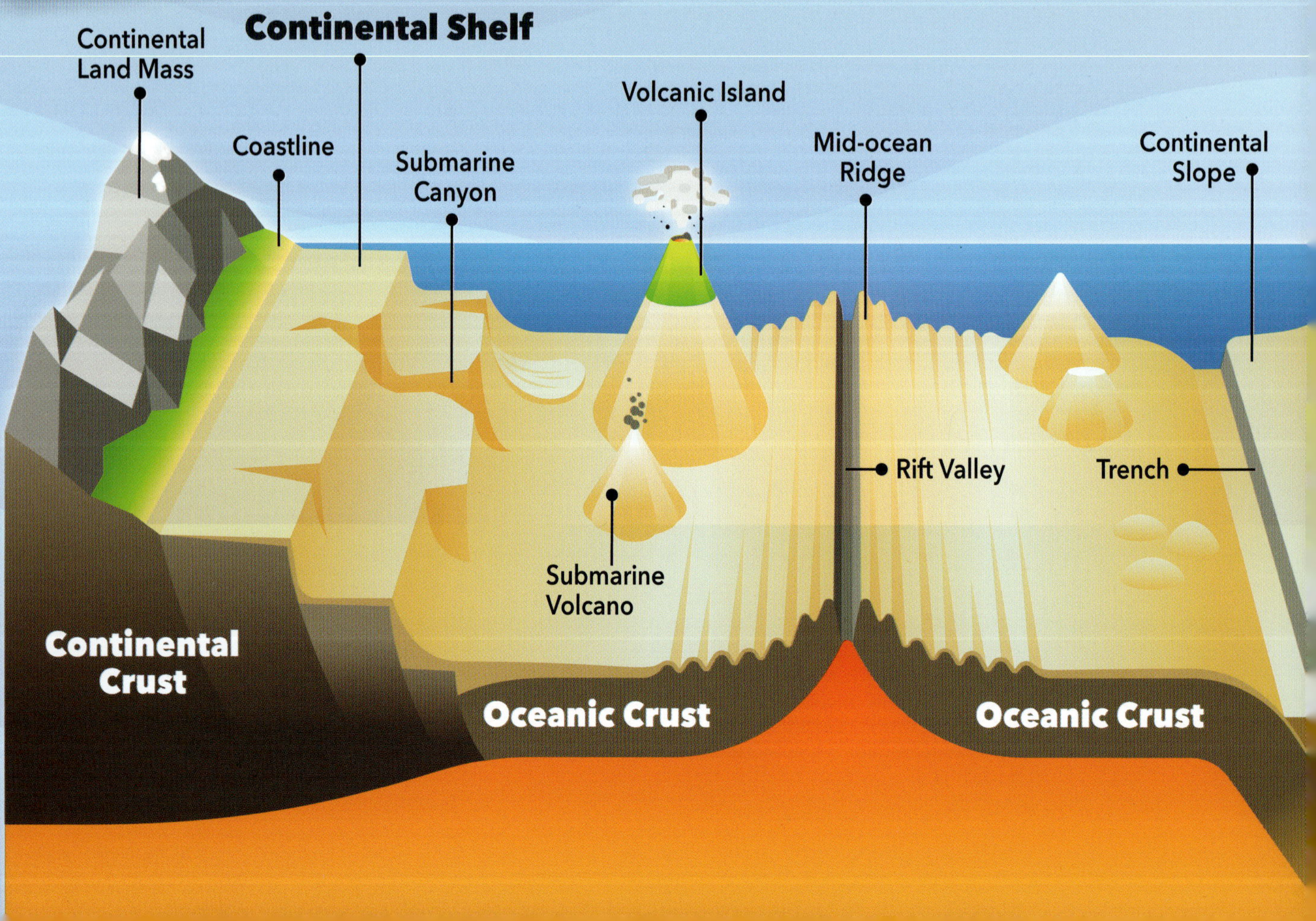

Continental Land Mass

Continental Shelf

Coastline

Submarine Canyon

Volcanic Island

Mid-ocean Ridge

Continental Slope

Rift Valley

Trench

Submarine Volcano

Continental Crust

Oceanic Crust

Oceanic Crust

Europe's Boundaries

At an ocean boundary, a nation has control over the ocean and the continental shelf for a distance of 200 nautical miles from the shore. This distance is set by member countries of the United Nations under the UNCLOS agreement.

1. Eastern Europe meets Asia along the Ural Mountains and the Caspian Sea
2. Northern Europe is bounded by the Arctic Ocean
3. Western Europe is bounded by the Atlantic Ocean
4. Southern Europe is bounded by the Mediterranean Sea

Asia

Europe

UNCLOS

The United Nations Convention on the Law of the Sea (UNCLOS) sets rules that countries use to determine who has control over the water and the seafloor at a nation's ocean boundary.

Continental Land Mass

Volcano

Continental Crust

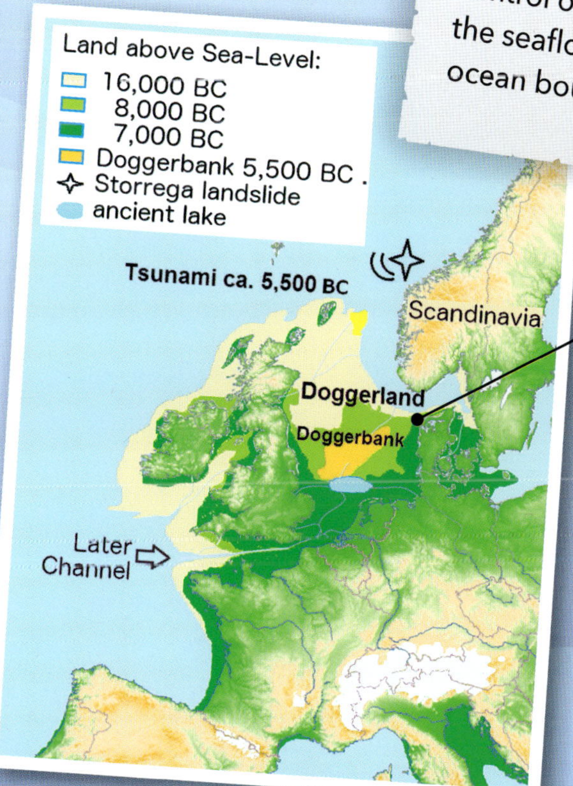

Doggerland

Thousands of years ago, the UK was connected to Europe by dry land. A section of this is called Doggerland. It was home to Stone Age people until rising sea levels forced them to move to higher ground. Doggerland is now a location for offshore oil and gas mining.

Continent of Europe

Where exactly is Europe?

Earth's continents do not have precise borders that everyone would agree with. We carefully define the borders of countries, but not of the continents on which they lie. Europe is entirely in the Northern Hemisphere.

Countries and Cities

There are 51 countries and independent states in Europe, although politics in some areas cause people to believe this number should be different.

Largest cities in Europe by population

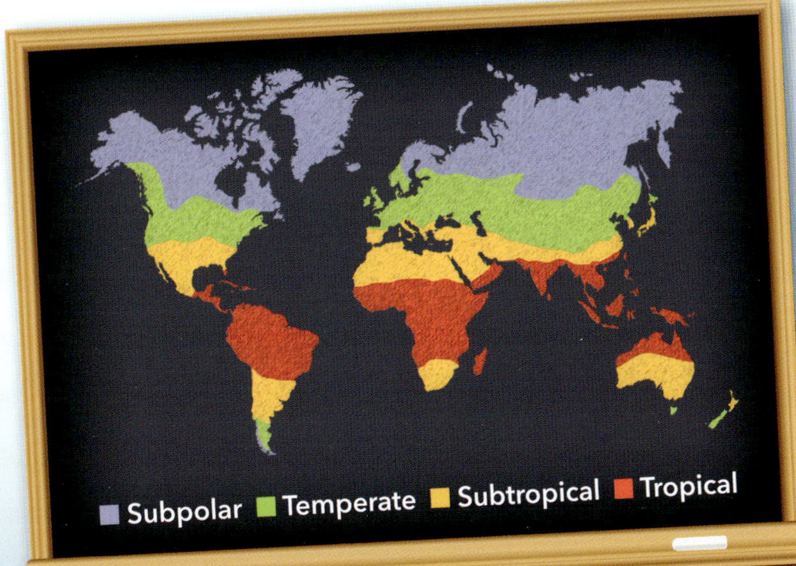

RUSSIA
GEORGIA
AZERBAIJAN
ARMENIA

Climate of Europe

Europe has an arctic climate in its far north and a Mediterranean climate in its far south. The term 'Mediterranean climate' is now used around the world to refer to a climate which features hot, dry summers and wet, mild winters. Snow during the winter is common throughout central and northern Europe, and at high altitudes in mountainous areas.

Istanbul, Turkey: Over 15 million people

Moscow, Russia: Over 12 million people

London, UK: Over 9 million people

Regions of Europe

Europe is usually thought of as having four separate regions, based on the four compass directions of north, south, west and east.

Western Europe

The islands of Great Britain and Ireland are in western Europe.

Southern Europe

This region includes the countries and islands in the area called the Mediterranean. The most populated countries in Southern Europe include Italy, Greece, Spain and Portugal.

Northern Europe

Northern Europe is covered with ice and snow during the winter. The most northerly parts of Europe are within the line of latitude called the Arctic Circle. Parts of northern Europe are only a few hundred kilometres from the North Pole.

Eastern Europe

Countries of the former Eastern Bloc and Soviet Union are included in Eastern Europe. Eastern Russia is located on the continent of Asia. Western Russia is located on the continent of Europe. Turkey also has land in the two continents of Europe and Asia.

Landscapes

High Mountains

The highest mountain in Europe is Mount Elbrus. This dormant volcano is in Russia and it is 5,600 metres high. Since Mount Elbrus is near the division between Europe and Asia, some people say that Mont Blanc, which lies between France and Italy, is really Europe's highest mountain, at 4,800 metres high.

Long Rivers

The longest river in Europe is the Volga River in Russia. The second longest river is the Danube River. It rises in Germany, then flows eastwards before it enters the Black Sea through a delta in Romania and Ukraine.

Flat Plains

Central Poland

The central plains of Europe extend across the continent and were once covered with forests. The plains are now sources of agricultural produce and also have very large human populations.

Deserts

Europe's deserts include the Deliblato Sands in Serbia, the Oltenian Sahara Desert in Romania, and the Tabernas Desert in Spain.

Tabernas Desert, Spain

Arctic tundra

Tundra

In the far north of Europe, there are plains called tundra. Beneath the tundra surface, there is a permanent layer of frozen ground called permafrost. In the winter, the treeless tundra is covered with snow.

A paaltjasker windmill in the Netherlands

Below Sea Level

In the Netherlands, also known as Holland, much of the coastal land is below sea level. Constant pumping out of the seawater is needed to keep these areas from being flooded. The Dutch windmills were needed in the past both to grind grain and to drain water from farmland. Today, there are massive flood gates to control the seawater.

European Organisations

NATO

The North Atlantic Treaty Organization fosters defence and security cooperation between its members, which include nations from North America and Europe. NATO strives for peaceful resolution of conflicts, but it also undertakes military operations.

European Union

In 1993, a number of European countries formed the European Union. This organisation promotes cooperation and trade amongst its members. In 2020, Britain withdrew from the EU in a process called Brexit, leaving 27 nations as members.

EURO

The EU has its own currency, the euro. This means that travellers across most of the member countries can use the same currency in all of them, waithout having to exchange their money for local coins and notes.

Volcanoes

Europe has both active and dormant volcanoes

Mount Etna

Located in Sicily, this active volcano produces smoke, rocks and lava.

Mount Vesuvius

The volcano which buried the ancient city of Pompeii, Italy, in AD 79.

Mount Elbrus

Located in Russia, this dormant volcano last erupted 2,000 years ago.

Santorini Volcano

The crater left by the huge explosion of the Santorini volcano in Greece, about 3,600 years ago, is now filled by seawater.

Eyjafjallajokul

This Icelandic volcano erupted in 2010, producing ash which spread across parts of Europe. Fagradalsfjall volcano is also in Iceland. It erupted with flows of lava in 2022.

The People of Europe

Living on a particular continent is one of the ways that people define themselves. People in Europe who call themselves Europeans mean that they have a history that is connected to the European place where they live or their ancestors came from.

How Many People?

The total population of Europe is 748 million.

The countries in Europe with the most people are Russia, Germany, Great Britain and France.

The smallest independent state in Europe, apart from Vatican City, is San Marino, with only about 34,000 people. San Marino is located within Italy.

Russia: Over 145 million people

San Marino: Over 34,000 people

Stone Age Humans

The Neanderthals were a prehistoric species of humans. They lived at the same time as our own human ancestors. Neanderthals were heavier than modern humans, and evidence of their Stone Age culture is still being discovered across Europe.

Religion in Europe

The main religion throughout Europe is Christianity, although people of all other religions also live there. The customs of the original folk religions of Europe are still followed in many areas.

Europe's Economy

Trade and the EU

The European Union of 27 countries has created a trading group that is one of the largest in the world. A large proportion of trade in the EU is amongst its own members. This provides benefits to small EU nations.

EXPORTS

Olive oil from Italy

Oranges from Spain

Wine from France

Vehicles from Germany

The Service Economy

The growing service economy in Europe includes tourism, social and financial services. The European banking industry provides services to customers around the world. The stability of nations in western Europe makes their banking services attractive to individuals as well as other countries.

High-tech

The development of high-tech industry in Europe has contributed to its reputation for being a source of reliable and innovative manufactured products. These include motor vehicles, industrial machinery and medical technology.

Agriculture

Despite its high degree of urbanisation, Europe still has very large areas of farmland and is a major producer of some crops. Europe's dairy products are renowned worldwide for their variety and quality.

Wildlife Wonders

Monkeys

There were once primates living in many parts of Europe. Today, the Barbary macaque of Gibraltar is the only non-human primate living in the wild in Europe.

Golden eagle

Forest Animals

In prehistoric times, large parts of Europe were covered with dense forests. The wildlife that evolved there includes the grey wolf, golden eagle, lynx and brown bear. The European bison is now extinct in the wild. The wolf in the fairy tale, *Red Riding Hood*, and the bears in *Goldilocks*, are all based on the wild animals of the European forests.

Grey wolf

Brown bear

Exporting Ferals

The foxes, stoats and rabbits that live in Europe were exported around the world to other countries when European explorers travelled around the globe from the 1700s onwards. These animals unfortunately have become feral pests in other countries, including Australia and New Zealand.

Cattle

The ancestor of all domestic cattle was the auroch. This animal is now extinct but it once used to live across Europe.

Camargue

The Camargue is an important wetland in southern France. Flamingoes and wild, white horses roam the Camargue. They are one of the oldest breeds of horses in the world.

Special Places in Europe

❶ Acropolis

Located on a hilltop in Athens, Greece, the Acropolis dates from about 2,500 years ago. It is important as a centre where the political system of democracy was born.

❷ Stonehenge

Located in southern England, Stonehenge is an ancient stone circle built thousands of years ago in the Stone Age as a religious and cultural centre for the local people.

3 Vatican City

Although it is located within Italy, Vatican City is a separate and independent state. Headed by the Pope, who resides at the Vatican, Roman Catholicism is the world's leading Christian religion. Latin is one of the languages still used for daily communication in Vatican City.

4 Eiffel Tower

The Eiffel Tower in Paris, France, was meant to be a temporary structure, built to commemorate the 100-year anniversary of the French Revolution. However, Parisians loved it so much that they decided to keep it. The Eiffel Tower is now recognised by billions of people around the world as a symbol of Paris.

⑤ The Alps

A mountain range in western Europe, The Alps are renowned for their beauty.

⑥ Castles

European medieval castles have inspired many fairy tales and works of art. They even provided ideas for a number of Disney cartoons, and for castles built in Disney theme parks around the world.

7 Black Forest

Located in Germany, the Black Forest is a mountain region famed for its dense pine forests and examples of traditional German buildings. Cuckoo clocks and Black Forest cake are two creations from this region that are enjoyed by people in countries far away from Germany. The Grimm brothers' fairy tales were often set in places inspired by the Black Forest area.

6 *Neuschwanstein Castle, Germany*

8 Mont Saint Michel

Mont Saint Michel is a small island in Normandy, France, but it is only surrounded by water at high tide. The abbey on the summit dates from the 700s. A similar island exists off the coast of Cornwall in England. It is called Saint Michael's Mount.

Northern Lights

The Aurora Borealis is a stunning natural light display in the sky. The lights appear in broad, coloured bands from areas close to the North Pole. They are caused by gases reacting to the Earth's magnetic field.

Mediterranean

The coastlines where European countries meet the Mediterranean Sea are places of popular beaches, as well as ports for shipping. Some of the world's largest shipping businesses operate from ports along the coast.

Glossary

Arctic Circle northern line of latitude around the Earth

Arctic climate climate with long, very cold winters and short, cool summers

aurochs extinct animals that were the ancestors of modern cattle breeds

democracy system of government in which people vote for their leaders

dormant volcano inactive volcano that may erupt at some time in the future

Eastern Bloc group of communist countries in eastern Europe

folk religion religious beliefs and practices that are not part of centralised religions

Ice Age one of many periods in Earth's history when ice and snow covered very large areas and sea levels were lower than today

Permafrost is a frozen layer of subsoil that never defrosts

The Stone Age was a prehistoric era when human ancestors only used stone tools

innovative having inventive ideas and activities

Mediterranean climate climate which features hot, dry summers and wet, mild winters

nautical mile term used to measure distance over water or when travelling in the air. It measures 1.85 kilometres

North Pole northern point where the lines of longitude meet

Northern Hemisphere part of the Earth that is north of the Equator

ocean abyss very deep part of an ocean

permafrost frozen layer of subsoil that never defrosts

plate tectonics movement of large blocks of land across the Earth

river delta wetlands that form as rivers empty their water into another body of water, such as an ocean, lake, or another river

Stone Age prehistoric era when human ancestors only used stone tools

tundra flat, treeless plains in cold regions

urbanisation moving to cities

Mount Elbrus

Index

The Vatican p:27

Stonehenge